TO NATIVITY AND BEYOND!

Christmas Plays and Other Dramas for All-age Audiences

by

Donna Vann

First published in 2022 by Slow Gecko Books.

© 2022 by Donna Vann. All rights reserved.

The right of Donna Vann to be identified as the author of this work has been asserted by her in accordance with the Copyright, Designs and Patents Act, 1988 (United Kingdom).

No part of this publication may be reproduced, performed, stored or transmitted in any form or by any means without prior written permission of the author, except as follows:

Permission is granted to the original purchaser of this book to photocopy scripts for actors, and to perform the dramas royalty-free if no admission is charged. If tickets are sold, please contact the author via her website for further information: www.donnavann.com

Every precaution has been taken to verify the accuracy of the information contained in this book; the author assumes no responsibility for any errors or omissions. No liability is assumed for damages that may result from the use of this material.

ISBN: 978-1-7391449-0-6

Cover and design by Julienne Durber

Cover photo from NASA's James Webb Space Telescope

CONTENTS

NATIVITY DRAMAS

THE LOST CAMEL – 10 minutes   9
Yasmin hates sand! She and her very contrary camel are lost in the desert; the Magi have vanished, and she can't even see the bright star. But when the Angel Gabriel appears to show her the promised baby, she can't wait to tell her friends.

TIME TRAVELLING AT CHRISTMAS – 15 minutes   17
Teens Jess and Sam are devastated – they hoped to visit the future but their Time Travelometer has sent them to the year 3 AD! Led by their Guide to Christmas Past, Present and Future, they discover something even more mind-bending than time travel.

A VERY SPECIAL BABY – 20 minutes   27
Isaiah conducts the audience through extraordinary encounters from the desert all the way to the stable at Bethlehem, to meet a very special baby.

SHORT DRAMAS FOR CHURCH OR YOUTH GROUPS

THE BOX   47
A group of friends discover God is so much more than a large purple box.

ADAM AND EVIE   53
Eden Zoo's Boss warned Adam and Evie not to let the snake out of its cage, but the snake is very convincing!

OUT OF OUR COMFORT(S) ZONE   59
Staying with a family in a Cambodian village, Jamie and Bethany are shocked by the lack of creature comforts – and by the strong faith of their Christian hosts.

BE KIND, REWIND   65
The angels at Trainee Angel School are frustrated they don't have much influence over their assigned humans. Then one angel decides to borrow God's emergency remote control, with surprising consequences!

AN EASTER MEDITATION

"I REMEMBER ..."   73
Fictional character Abigail, one of Jesus' nieces, reflects back on the scene in the Upper Room the night her uncle died.

PRAISE FOR THE PLAYS

I was privileged to work with the highly talented Donna Vann while I was Assistant Curate at St Faith's Church, Lee-on-the-Solent. We asked Donna to write a script for our *Live Nativity* in 2019 and she produced not one but several, on different themes, with actors placed in stations across the church. The scripts in action were electric, witty, modern, engaging, and produced much delight and laughter. They drew great numbers of new people into church. Donna has added some further excellent scripts to the ones we road-tested with such success and I have no doubt that this book will be a tremendous asset for any church or youth group.

Here is some of the feedback we received:

"A fabulous event."

"I'm still buzzing!"

"What an amazing accomplishment."

"A Christmas message that will stay in the memory."

"Truly an amazing epic! Thank you, thank you."

"Really creative....not what I expected."

"I was very moved by the rapt expression of the children taking it all in."

"It was fantastic to see a huge number of families come along and the children so fully absorbed in the dramas."

"A great success....I truly believe it touched people's lives."

31 August 2022

Revd Dr Mary Kells
Currently Chaplain at King's College, Cambridge

WHY "BEYOND"?

Let's take Christmas *beyond* the church, beyond cute little shepherds wearing tea towels on their heads, to reach the wider community. The birth of Jesus was an event in history. Magi came looking for him – Herod tried in vain to destroy him – angels heralded him and shepherds worshipped him.

The goal of these dramas is to entertain, but also to prompt questions: why all the fuss about a baby born in humble circumstances over 2000 years ago? Does this event impact our modern lives – or me personally?

"Beyond" also refers to the other short dramas, four for any season and one for Easter. Most of the scripts in this book have been tested in performance.

Nativity Dramas

These were produced for all-age audiences at St Faith's Church, Lee-on-the-Solent, Hampshire, alongside a "Live Nativity" event with real animals. Actors were a mix of adults, teens and children. Occasionally we were able to have a live baby Jesus onstage, which was quite moving, if a bit tricky! The plays can also be performed by youth groups.

During partial lockdown we produced a film which featured actors in family groups; some of "Time Travelling at Christmas" was adapted from "Your King Has Come!" which can be watched by visiting St Faith's Church Youtube channel and searching for Your King has Come.

Short Dramas for Family Church

The first plays in this section were developed with Xplosion Drama Club, an enthusiastic group of 11-14's at Knowle Parish Church in the West Midlands. They are designed to be performed at a Family Service and last no more than ten minutes. Youth groups could also use them to spark discussions.

Additionally, there is an Easter meditation.

Genders and names can be changed as needed. American groups should feel free to adapt British phrases!

Thank you

Many heartfelt thanks go to Margaret Fulford, who taught me so much about directing plays and working with young people. To Revd Dr Paul Chamberlain, Vicar at St Faith's Church, for fostering creativity, and to Revd Dr Mary Kells, Executive Producer extraordinaire! To the scores of actors and behind-the-scenes workers who threw themselves into making sure that costumes, setting, lighting and other details came together on the day.

A big thank-you to Cherith Baldry for helpful editorial input and to Julienne Durber for his expertise in all things technical. Also to Tim Hooper for Nativity images, and to Elina Platner, Dave Vann and Millay Vann for their part in making this book happen. And of course to my husband Roger, my First Reader, life Stage Manager and encourager, who provided the title.

Donna Vann

NATIVITY DRAMAS

THE LOST CAMEL

SCENE: Somewhere in the desert east of Bethlehem; curtains onstage are closed

Persian servant Yasmin [or Farzin if male]
Camel [or camel prop]
Angel Gabriel
Angel 1
Angel 2
Manger Tableau, non-speaking: Mary, Joseph, Baby, Magi, Shepherd etc. as space allows

[YASMIN enters with CAMEL from behind audience, grumbling, paces in front of curtain]

YASMIN: "Follow that star, follow that star ..." I haven't seen that big star in ages! *[to camel]* It's all *your* fault we got lost in the sandstorm!

[CAMEL brays]

YASMIN: I'm sorry, but you're a camel! You should know your way through the desert!

[CAMEL brays]

YASMIN: Haven't seen hide nor hair of my master, Sir Caspar, and the other Magi. Where is everyone? Sand, sand and more sand – me, I'm a city girl. So when Sir Caspar says, "Yasmin, we're leaving Persia and going on a journey," I says, "Somewhere exciting?" and he says, "We're heading west! To find the promised baby."

YASMIN: And I says, "We got plenty of babies in Persia," and he says, "Not like this one, we don't." So I says to Sir Caspar, how will we know which way to go? And he says, we got to follow this super-bright star. So we did. Miles and miles and miles. Did I mention I don't like tents? Or sand? Or smelly camels!

[CAMEL brays]

YASMIN: Now here's the thing. Did you know you can get *clouds* in the desert? Yep, and what happens when you get clouds? *[ask audience]* Can you see the stars? NO! YOU CAN'T SEE THE STARS! Did Sir Caspar and his friends do a risk assessment before they set out? "Distance: 1000 miles, no Satnav, no street lamps, number of possible cloudy nights" – Nope! They said, "We will be led." And we were. Until me and my *trusty camel* ...

[CAMEL brays]

YASMIN: ... got lost in a sandstorm!

[YASMIN paces in worry, pauses]

YASMIN: Sir Caspar worships an unknown God. The so-called "God above all gods". When I ask, "Who is this God," he says, "That's what we're going on a journey to find out." Sometimes I don't understand a word he says. And now we're lost. Did I mention, it's all *your* fault?

[CAMEL brays]

YASMIN: Do you see a star? Does anyone see a star?

[STAR appears for several seconds, audience will call out. YASMIN doesn't see it]

YASMIN: Wait a minute, wait a minute – Sir Caspar used to recite a poem – it was something like this:

"Twinkle, twinkle little star" – no, that's not it –
"O big bright light" – No. I've got it!

"O blessed light" – that's it! You say it with me, so I don't forget.

"O blessed light."
[gets audience to repeat]

Right. Then it goes: "We seek you through the darkest night."
[gets audience to repeat]

The end bit is: "Come, shine upon us."
[gets audience to repeat]

There! We've said the poem! Now where is that star?

[YASMIN keeps looking around but misses the STAR when it briefly appears]

YASMIN:	I give up. Let's turn back.

[CAMEL brays and shakes head "no"]

[YASMIN puts camel down and sits in discouragement on a pile of cushions, left. Spotlight on ANGEL GABRIEL who appears from behind curtain, right, moves to centre in front of curtain]

GABRIEL:	Yasmin!
YASMIN:	*[screams, jumps up]* Who are you?
GABRIEL:	I am the angel Gabriel.
YASMIN:	How do you know my name?
GABRIEL:	I've been sent to you by the Most High God, who made you and loves you.
YASMIN:	What? No – no no no – I must be having one of them desert vision things – what's it called – a mirage! You're just a mirage! Something I made up in my head. Go away!

[CAMEL brays warningly]

GABRIEL:	Yasmin, I am not a mirage.
YASMIN:	*[Stuffs fingers in her ears]* Not listening! Go away!
GABRIEL:	*[patiently]* Yasmin, you were led to the right place. Your master is already here, at the birth of the promised baby.

[STAR appears and stays on until end]

YASMIN:	*[looks around, puzzled, reacts as she sees the star]* Where?

[CHIMES sound as ANGELS pull back curtains to reveal manger tableau, spotlit]

YASMIN:	Wow! *[pause as she takes in the scene]* Not a mirage?

[CAMEL brays "no" and GABRIEL shakes head]

YASMIN:	So – that means – *[pointing to Gabriel]* – you're really an – angel?

[CAMEL brays "yes" and GABRIEL nods]

YASMIN:	Oh sorry, really sorry! Uh, where were we?
GABRIEL:	At the birth of the promised baby!

YASMIN: But who is this promised baby?

ANGEL 1: He's the light of the world.

ANGEL 2: The bright and morning star.

ANGEL 1: Wonderful counsellor, our Prince of Peace.

ANGEL 2: Son of the Most High God.

ANGEL 1: He has come to save and forgive you.

GABRIEL: Worship the baby Jesus!

[YASMIN moves into manger, slowly takes in scene, bows in worship]

YASMIN: I think I get it. God has come down to *our* world, with all its smelly camels and sand and people who don't understand ... he's here! *[awed, she comes out to face audience]* It makes me feel like singing! Will you sing with me?

[MUSIC – A short version of "It was on a Starry Night" or other familiar Christmas song. ANGELS lead audience in singing; during the song, the MAGI set their gifts in front of the manger]

YASMIN: Sometimes we have to leave our safe homes and go on a journey, to find the truth. It was worth traipsing through the lonely, sandy desert to meet this promised baby. Jesus. Light of the World. Son of the Most High. *[pause]* I've got to tell my friends!

[MUSIC as YASMIN grabs CAMEL and rushes off past the audience, followed by procession of MAGI]

Production Notes for "The Lost Camel"

STAGING: This was performed in a medium-sized room in conjunction with a "Live Nativity" event, for which time slots were booked. Groups of about 30 viewed the performance, following a one-way system to enter the theatre and exiting to see the live animals. To avoid actor burn-out we used two groups of actors.

The drama could also be presented in a larger auditorium, having Yasmin stay down with the audience until the stable tableau.

ACTORS: one actor who can interact with the audience in a lively way, plus a "camel", which could be a person in costume or mask, or a prop. A kazoo makes an excellent braying sound, which can be done by someone just offstage. In addition, there are three small speaking parts and a flexible number of non-speaking parts.

SCENE: Audience sits inside a simulated Bedouin tent, with a curtain covering stable tableau to be revealed at the end. If the performance space doesn't have a curtain, a large portable Zoom curtain is handy. Star is above and behind the manger, visible to audience but only when lit up. Alternatively it could be on a long pole which a tableau actor raises or lowers as needed. If no screen is available, words to the song can be on a glittery flip chart turned by angels.

PROPS:
Camel
Kazoo for camel bray
Manger
Star
Screen or flip chart

TIME TRAVELLING AT CHRISTMAS

SCENE: A raised platform to one side of stage which is bare, except for a single chair

Guide to Christmas Past/Present/Future
Sam
Jess
Herod
Guard
Mum
Mary
Joseph
Donkey
Gabriel
Wise Ones (mostly non-speaking)
Adult Jesus and children (non-speaking)

[GUIDE waits on platform, looking all around, occasionally checking electronic watch. Flash of light; teens SAM and JESS roll onto platform as if dropped from the sky. JESS carries the Time Travelometer]

SAM: Did it work?

JESS: It did!

[BOTH excitedly high-five]

SAM: Did we make it to the future?

JESS: Must have. We set the Time Travelometer for the year 5000.

SAM: How can we know for sure? *[Sees Guide]* Pardon me, can you please tell me what year this is?

GUIDE: Hm, so polite, very good! It is *[consults watch]* the Year five thousand, five hundred and nine.

[SAM and JESS jump with excitement]

JESS: We did it!

SAM: Five thousand, five hundred and nine! We're in the future!

[BOTH look around in amazement]

GUIDE: *[checks watch]* According to the Byzantine calendar, that is. *You* would call it the Year 3 AD.

SAM: Year wha'?

JESS: So, we went back to the *past*?

SAM: Oh, no!

[BOTH hugely disappointed]

GUIDE: You'll have to make the best of it. Anyway, I've been waiting for you!

BOTH: You have?

GUIDE: That's right. *[importantly]* Sam, and Jess, *[nods at each]* I have been sent to help you.

JESS: Who are you?

GUIDE: All you need to know is, I am on a Cosmic Mission to guide you into the story!

SAM: What story is that?

GUIDE: A story that encompasses the past, present and future. *[puts on hat with a flourish]* Ahem! I am your Guide to Christmas Past!

[BOTH shrug, unimpressed]

JESS: O-kay ... What do you mean, you're our guide?

GUIDE: All will be revealed! *[claps hands three times]*

[MUSIC begins, WISE ONES process in from behind audience, looking all around at the sky. STAR appears over the stage and remains visible to end. JESS and SAM watch scene with interest]

WISE ONES: *[randomly, not in unison]* Look! The star, the star!

[As they near the front, HEROD and his GUARD enter onstage. WISE ONES move to one side for whispered consultation as HEROD speaks. WISE ONES react to what they hear with whispered distress]

HEROD: *[pacing back and forth, in pain]* Arrgh! My head hurts! The rumours say there's a *new* King of the Jews! I, Herod, am King of the Jews! Always people plotting behind my back, trying to take me down....

GUARD:	Don't forget my lord, you have two thousand bodyguards, including us trusty Celts!
HEROD:	Yes, yes – NO! Trust no one. They're all out to kill me! My spies have told me – somewhere in Judea, a special baby is about to be born. *[scornfully]* A Messiah!
GUARD:	My lord, calm yourself.
HEROD:	*[explosive]* This is me being calm!! *[sits]*
GUARD:	Here, my lord. *[hands beaker]* This will ease your pains.
HEROD:	*[Drinks]* Where is this baby? Where is he? *[stands and paces]* I can't allow him to grow up and become King of the Jews. We must take action!
GUARD:	Of course, my lord. But – ahem – what action will you take against a – baby?
HEROD:	Who asked you? We must find him, before it's too late.
GUARD:	But my lord –
HEROD:	Go!

[GUARD bows to Herod and exits. WISE ONES exit quickly. During next lines HEROD paces, looking furious]

JESS:	Of course, this is the Nativity story! Baby Jesus was born, and King Herod was all upset, because he thought the baby was going to take over his throne.
GUIDE:	Very good! You obviously paid attention in Religious Studies! *[looks sternly at SAM who shrugs apologetically]*

[HEROD exits]

SAM:	The baby will be okay, won't he?
GUIDE:	Let's not get ahead of ourselves! Oh look, here come our hero and heroine. Although, pretty soon the story will have another hero!

[SAM looks bewildered, JESS thoughtful. MARY and JOSEPH enter from behind audience, leading reluctant DONKEY. They are aware of actors on platform but mostly ignore them]

GUIDE: *[consults watch, to Mary and Joseph]* Move along, we're on a timetable! We still have Christmas Present and Christmas Future to come.

JOSEPH: Excuse me, but have you ever tried to lead a donkey?

[JOSEPH tugs on rope, DONKEY brays stubbornly]

GUIDE: The donkey is really important!

DONKEY: *[escapes JOSEPH, speaks to audience]* Hee-haw, I'm really important!

[During the following JOSEPH manages to grab DONKEY and bring it back]

JESS: I don't get it, why would a donkey be important?

[DONKEY brays, annoyed]

GUIDE: *[digs in bag, brings out scroll, rolls it back and forth]* The prophecy is here somewhere – "He will be called, Wonderful, Counsellor, Prince of Peace..." No, nothing about a donkey there – *[rolls through scroll in frustration]*

[GABRIEL appears onstage and steps forward. MARY, JOSPEH and DONKEY gasp in fear and move back]

GABRIEL: I will tell you why the donkey is important.

[MARY and JOSEPH listen, DONKEY trots over and flops down in front of Gabriel, staring up expectantly]

GABRIEL: *[dramatically]* The donkey is important, because the baby Mary is about to have, will be a king! He will be so powerful that he could blow you over with his breath! *[mimes blowing breath]*

[MARY and JOSEPH lean back, DONKEY brays in fear, falls in a heap]

GABRIEL: *[holds up one finger]* But –

DONKEY: *[stands up]* But, the king rides a donkey because he comes in peace! *[looks around, puzzled]* Did I say that?

GABRIEL: You did! Well done, O clever Donkey!

[DONKEY brays with pride and prances around]

GUIDE: Move along, we must keep going!

[MARY, JOSEPH and DONKEY scurry back several paces and begin again. During the following lines they walk forward and turn to face the audience]

MARY: Where are we, Joseph? I'm so tired. And cold.

JOSEPH: I know, my love. Bethlehem is just beyond the next hill. *[points towards stage]* We can't stop now. We don't want our baby to be born in the middle of the desert!

MARY: You say "our baby", but he's not really ours, is he?

JOSEPH: You're right, Mary. Our baby belongs to God. "He will save people from their sins" – that's what the angel told me. What a privilege, to be parents of the Messiah!

MARY: I wish privilege wasn't so tiring. And I can't help thinking – what if the people don't want a Messiah?

DONKEY: *[to audience]* Hee-haw, what's a Messiah?

[Exit JOSEPH and MARY, dragging DONKEY. Meanwhile GUIDE returns scroll to bag]

SAM: But Jesus was born centuries ago. Why do *we* need to know this story?

GUIDE: Watch and you will see. *[changes hats, taps watch]* I am your Guide to Christmas Present!

JESS: *[rolls eyes]* Really?

[Jess' MUM storms onstage, wearing paper Christmas crown and carrying a duster, begins dusting frantically]

MUM: Jess! Jess, where are you?

JESS: *[pauses, uncertain what to do]* Mum?

MUM: Come down here! What are you dawdling up there for? You need to clean your room!

JESS: *[joins Mum onstage]* Clean my room? Mum, you don't understand, *[gestures at Guide]* I'm in the middle of a Cosmic Mission here!

MUM: *[stressed]* We don't have time for cosmic missions! It's Christmas Eve! We've got the neighbours coming round, and you know we always play Dad's favourite board game and watch 'It's a Wonderful Life' together!

JESS: *[mimes 'Boring!' to Sam]* Mum – this is why I don't like Christmas! It's having to be nice to weird neighbours and acting like we're a lovey-dovey family, when we hardly get along the rest of the year!

MUM: I'm sure you're exaggerating. *[sternly]* Now will you please get a move on! *[exits, dusting bits of stage on the way]*

[JESS returns to platform]

SAM: My parents are always so stressed getting ready for Christmas. I don't know why they bother.

JESS: I did love doing the Nativity play at school. I always wanted to be Mary or an angel, but usually I was stuck being the donkey.

[DONKEY runs on]

DONKEY: The donkey is REALLY important!

[JOSEPH drags DONKEY off, DONKEY brays]

SAM: *[to Guide]* What you showed us – I mean what our "Guide to Christmas Past" showed us – it doesn't seem to fit with the Nativity story.

JESS: That's right, you hear about the first Christmas and it's all fluffy sheep and angels – but really, they were exhausted, they were in danger –

SAM: And what was all that stuff about the Messiah? I don't remember that.

GUIDE: Oh, it was there. You just didn't notice. *[changes to Christmas Past hat, taps watch, claps hands three times]*

[MUSIC plays as JOSEPH and MARY enter onstage, joyous, carrying baby, followed by DONKEY. MARY sits. WISE ONES follow making an admiring semi-circle behind them and offer their gifts one by one. GABRIEL appears and stands to one side.]

GABRIEL: All this happened as God foretold. Baby Jesus was born, the Son of the Most High God, the Messiah promised for centuries. King Jesus came to give us new life, starting with you – *[gestures to people in manger scene]* and you – *[gestures to Sam and Jess]* and you! *[gestures to audience]* But now it's time for Mary and Joseph to escape to Egypt, to get away from Herod.

[MARY bundles up baby, DONKEY leads JOSEPH, now in a hurry; they exit quickly past audience. Meanwhile GUIDE changes to Present hat, taps watch]

GUIDE:	That explains it all quite nicely, don't you think?
SAM:	Not really.
JESS:	So, you're saying there's a way to connect Baby Jesus, the stable, the Wise Ones and all that, with our lives today? Can Jesus help us – can he help *me* – like when I get anxious or overwhelmed?
GUIDE:	An excellent question!
SAM:	But Jesus died thousands of years ago.
JESS:	Yeah, but he came back, don't you remember?
GUIDE:	*[nodding]* And...?
JESS:	Well, if Jesus is still here, and if he came to give us new life, like the angel said – who wouldn't want that? That's even better than time travel!
SAM:	*[sceptically]* Huh! *[pause]* You said there's a Guide to Christmas Future?
GUIDE:	*[quickly rummages in bag, pulls out third hat and puts it on]* I am your Guide to Christmas Future!
SAM:	Whatever. We've been trying to get to the future – can you make it happen?
GUIDE:	I certainly can. *[taps watch]* Any moment now –
JESS:	*[excited]* What year will it be?
GUIDE:	Only God knows the answer to that. When time and history come to an end, there will be feasting and dancing at the greatest Christmas celebration ever known!
SAM:	Bring it on!

[SAM and JESS brace themselves. Lively MUSIC introduces a spontaneous free dance. GUIDE, JESS and SAM jump into the scene. ALL join in, including finally HEROD who has to be shown dance steps by other cast members. JESUS, with scars visible on his palms, enters with some CHILDREN and joins the dance. Audience members can be encouraged to take part. ALL exit dancing past the audience, except for SAM and JESS who return to the platform, set the travelometer and wait expectantly]

Production Notes for "Time Travelling at Christmas"

ACTORS: Ten speaking parts plus a flexible number of non-speaking. Some doubling up is possible, for example Mum could also be one of the Wise Ones, changing back to Mum for the end dance.

PROPS:
Star
Cross outline over star
Time Travelometer
Guide's bag, containing scroll and hats
Electronic watch
Duster
Chair or stool (Herod's chair, furniture in Jess's room, Mary's chair in stable scene)
Gifts from Wise Ones

COSTUMES:
Three quirky hats for Guide
Donkey costume, mask or headgear
Gabriel halo, wings
Crowns for Herod, Wise Ones
Paper Christmas crown for Mum

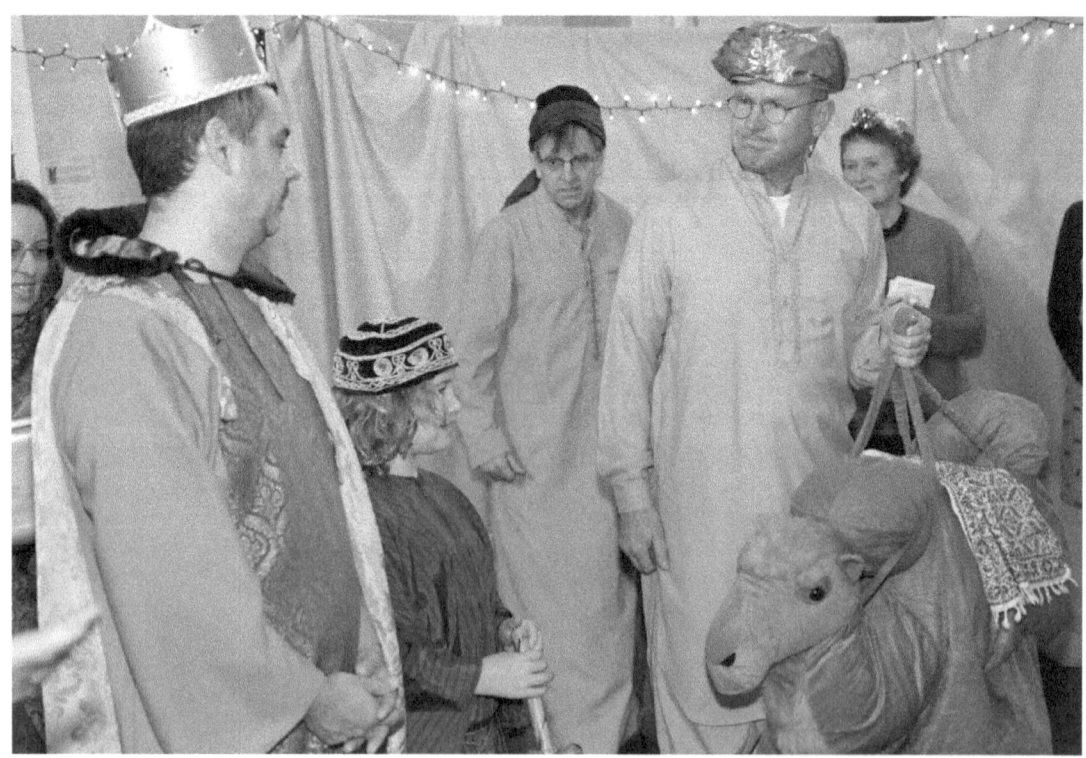

A VERY SPECIAL BABY

Narrator:
Prophet Isaiah

Inn Scene:
Tobias
Martha

Desert Scene:
Caspar
Melchior
Balthasar
Kir
Armita
Darius
Cas (a child)

Shepherd Scene:
Reuben
Seth
John
Nat
Sheep

Angel Scene:
Haniel
Kemuel
Uriel
Angels, non-speaking

Manger Scene (non-speaking):
Mary
Joseph
Baby
Shepherds, donkey, and so on. If using a small space, this scene also works well with simply the couple and their baby

[ISAIAH enters in front of closed curtains, carrying scroll. Plenty of ad lib and interaction with audience]

ISAIAH: Welcome! My name is Isaiah and I'm a prophet. Can anyone tell me what a prophet is? *[comments from audience]*

I'm from Jerusalem. Where do you live? *[comments from audience]* I've never heard of those places. You must be from the future! What is the year you're living in? *[does mental arithmetic]* Hmm, that means I lived nearly three thousand years before you!

Back then, God gave me messages to pass on to the Hebrew people. I told them they were like silly sheep, wandering away from God, ignoring what he said. Do you reckon that made me popular? *[comments from audience]* No, it didn't! That's the life of a prophet for you. But I had to go on telling the truth, even if no one wanted to hear it.

However, it wasn't all doom and gloom. I predicted that God would send a very special baby, the Messiah, a King who would also be a suffering servant – although how a King could be a servant who suffers was more than I knew. But I went on saying these things, year after year, because God told me to.

And finally, Messiah was born. Any guesses who that Messiah was? *[comments from audience]* How many years after my prophecy was Jesus the Messiah born? Want to take a guess? *[700]*

I've had a glimpse of the future, where you live – and I don't understand what I see. Is it true that people celebrate Messiah's birth by bringing trees into their homes? And the marketplace is overcrowded, with really awful music that blasts everyone's ears? "Jingle Bell Rock" – I don't even know what that means! Is it true that people dread the time of Messiah's birth? It was never meant to be like that.

Well, I managed to get myself into the future, so let's see if we can send you back to the past! Does that sound like a good idea? *[comments from audience]* You're about to travel over 2000 years back in time, to visit the first ever Christmas. We'll have to fly – so everyone spread out your arms – Here we go!

[MUSIC during the following]

ISAIAH: Over the seas – over the mountains – back in time – back, back, back – I see desert below! *[plops on floor]* We've landed! *[gets up]* Everyone okay? No bumps or bruises? *[looks around]* All I can see is sand but I think – *[listens]* – yes! Do you hear it?

SCENE ONE: Desert, somewhere east of Bethlehem

[WISE ONES and SERVANTS enter from left, CAS using shaker to imitate pace of camels. ARMITA carries a covered box containing gifts, DARIUS and KIR follow with camels]

WISE ONES:	*[chanting with energy]* So far – so far – follow the star!
SERVANTS:	*[flagging]* So far – so far – follow the star!
CAS:	Are we nearly there yet?
DARIUS:	I'm cold!
ARMITA:	I'm tired.
KIR:	I'm hungry!
CAS :	And me!
CASPAR:	Dawn is coming; we will camp here.
KIR:	*[to the other servants]* You do the tent, I'll see to the camels.

[WISE ONES sit by campfire, SERVANTS remain standing]

DARIUS:	We've been on the road from Persia for a month now – will we ever get there?
ARMITA:	And where is "there"? Remind me why we're doing this?
BALTHASAR:	It's our glorious quest!
MELCHIOR:	We must follow that star!
DARIUS:	Must we?
CASPAR:	Our life's work is to study the skies.
BALTHASAR:	There has never been such a star. Look how brightly it shines!
MELCHIOR:	This tells us that a very special baby has been born. We must go where the star leads, to celebrate his birth.
KIR:	Wait – you're saying, *you* don't know where we're going?
DARIUS:	*[runs around frantically]* We're lost in the desert! Doomed!
MELCHIOR:	You must trust the stars, my son, and the God who made them.

CASPAR: *[to ARMITA, imperiously]* Bring my pack.

[ARMITA bows, sets box centre stage and removes cover. She will bring out each gift and hold it up as mentioned]

BALTHASAR: These are our gifts for the special baby. Gold because he's a King.

SERVANTS: Ooooo!

CASPAR: Frankincense because he's God's Holy Priest.

SERVANTS: Ooooo!

DARIUS: A king, a priest, sounds like he's rich! Maybe we'll finally get to sleep on a soft bed in a palace, instead of the hard ground.

BALTHASAR: We believe he's more than a ruler living in luxury. Our stars tell us, this special baby brings hope.

CASPAR: He brings light for a dark world.

KIR: I don't get it.

BALTHASAR: It's a mystery!

MELCHIOR: So is the third gift. Myrrh. It signifies death.

SERVANTS: *[more muted]* Ooooo.

ARMITA: Death! Sounds like a rubbish gift!

CASPAR: But this death creates life.

MELCHIOR: The special baby will grow up to be a man, and then die. In dying, he will bring life for all people on earth.

DARIUS: We don't understand.

CASPAR: Neither do we!

BALTHASAR: It's a mystery.

MELCHIOR: That's why we're making this long journey. To understand, and to worship him.

CAS: Mysteries make me sleepy!

DARIUS: And me!

[ALL yawn and settle down for sleep]

ISAIAH: *[tiptoes away]* Shh, we don't want to wake them. Our next stop is a house in a village near Jerusalem. *[peeks behind curtain]* Hmm, Tobias looks a bit grumpy, but I suspect he's always like that.

SCENE TWO: Yard of a small inn, bright star above

[MARTHA and TOBIAS in front of their house, MARTHA sweeping. They interact with the audience]

TOBIAS:	What! More people? Go away!
MARTHA:	Sorry me darlings, we're all full up! You can't get a room in Bethlehem for love nor shekels! You ask me why? I'll tell you why – 'cos our glorious emperor Caesar decided it, that's why!
TOBIAS:	My cousin's got a goat pen you can use, for the right price. Do you mind sleeping with goats?
MARTHA:	Or you could sleep in the bed with our five kids and me mother-in-law. I'll warn you though, she snores.
TOBIAS:	Us Jews are fed up with them Romans! Caesar decided he wanted to count everyone. That's government for you, just one silly scheme after another. Everyone has to go back to the town where they was born for this census thing. That's why the inn is full up, plus every spare barn and stable. Guess I shouldn't grumble –
MARTHA:	But you will! *[leans in to audience]* Come closer – I'll tell you a secret – don't repeat this, you didn't hear it from me, right? Them Romans, they may be in charge now, but one day, we Jews'll be laughing! You ask me why? I'll tell you why! 'Cos we're getting a King! That's right, you heard me – a King! Someone on our side, who'll fight our corner.
TOBIAS:	A Jewish King, a Messiah. What d'you think about that! He's going to wipe out them Romans! I reckon he'll just say BOO! and they'll all run away.
MARTHA:	I felt right sorry for that couple with the donkey – it's cold and they looked so tired, and the wife was – you know. *[indicates large stomach]* We put them in our stable and I called the midwife, least we could do. She's just sent word, the baby's come, a healthy, bonny boy. Reckon I'll nip over and see the little'un when me work's done.
TOBIAS:	Funny thing, there's a blinding-bright star right over our stable. Wonder what that's about? Oh well, what are you lot gawping at? We've got an inn full of customers, can't stand here gossiping. Come on, Wife!
ISAIAH:	We're obviously not wanted here! Tell you what, we'll head for the hills.

SCENE THREE: Night, a hillside near Bethlehem

[SHEEP are restless, baa-ing]

REUBEN: *[Moves his staff close to them in a soothing way]* Calm down, calm down.

SETH: Beautiful clear night.

REUBEN: Cold!

SETH: Better cold than rain.

REUBEN: The flock's settled. You get some rest – I'll keep watch.

[SETH pulls his cloak around and gets ready to lie down]

SETH: Hope Nat and John are all right, over there with the other flock.

REUBEN: Them lads are dozy and that's a fact.

[LADS run in, speechless and out of breath]

JOHN: Seth!

NAT: Reuben!

SETH: *[jumps up]* What is it! Did you see lions? Tigers? Bears?

[SHEEP become agitated and baa louder]

REUBEN: *[to sheep]* Calm down, calm down.

JOHN: No! No lions.

NAT: No bears. It was – it was –

SETH: Tell it slowly.

NAT: You tell 'em.

JOHN: I'll tell 'em.

NAT: Well go on, tell 'em!

JOHN: I am telling 'em!

SETH and **REU**: So tell us!

JOHN:	So we was watching the sheep –
REUBEN:	Sleeping, more like.
SETH:	Or larking about.
NAT:	And the whole sky lit up!
JOHN:	Oi, I'm telling it! Nearly knocked us down, the light was so bright. We looked up – and you won't believe what we saw! White fluffy things!
SETH:	White fluffy things?
NAT:	In the sky! Angels!
JOHN:	*I* wanted to say that! The sky was full of white flying things.
SETH:	White fluffy things weren't angels, ye daft so-and-so, they was sheep!
NAT:	Flying sheep?
JOHN:	No, for sure they was angels. Singing!
REUBEN:	You lads got too much imagination. If there was any angels around, they wouldn't show theirselves to the likes of you, would they?
NAT:	But they did, honest!
SETH:	I reckon you saw some of them Unidentified Flying Objects. Not angels!
REUBEN:	Hey! You left the flock all by theirselves?
JOHN:	We had to! The angels told us to go –
NAT:	To Bethlehem –
JOHN:	To see the baby our prophets told us about!
NAT:	This is so big!
SETH:	A big baby? Bigger than a sheep? Like a camel?
JOHN:	No, a normal-sized baby. A very special baby.
NAT:	A baby with a mission!

JOHN: A *reeeally big* mission!

[Both NAT and JOHN stretch their arms out wide. SETH and REUBEN shake their heads]

NAT: Come with us – the angels'll explain it better than we can.

[ANGELS begin humming offstage]

JOHN: Come on!

[SHEPHERDS run off, motioning audience to follow]

ISAIAH: Well, they've obviously seen something exciting! Let's follow them and find out.

SCENE FOUR: Night, another hillside

[ISAIAH makes shushing motions to audience. ANGELS ignore audience. KEMUEL has a guitar]

HANIEL: Do you think those shepherds got the message?

URIEL: I don't know, humans are really thick.

KEMUEL: Can't understand why the Boss is so patient with them.

URIEL: That's how he is.

HANIEL: And loving. Remember how he promised to send the special baby, the one who would rescue the world?

URIEL: And now the Boss has come *himself* as the baby!

KEMUEL: Born in a cow stall instead of a palace. That's going above and beyond.

URIEL: And having us announce the birth to some smelly shepherds, before we tell anyone else!

HANIEL: They live in sheep poo, of course they smell!

KEMUEL: One thing puzzles me. I know because the Boss decided it, it's right. But why does the world need rescuing?

URIEL: Because humans mess up.

HANIEL: They forget about the Boss; they wander away from him.

URIEL: They're desperate for forgiveness.

KEMUEL: Humans are hopeless! If I were human, I would *never* mess up or forget about the Boss.

URIEL and HAN: *[they pause and stare at him]* Oh yes you would!

URIEL: You'd be just the same as they are. We all would.

HANIEL: You're right, though – humans need hope. This special baby brings hope for every person, no matter how often they fail.

URIEL: *[looking at Kemuel]* There's even hope for silly angels.

KEMUEL: Look sharp, they're here!

[ALL ANGELS stand with arms outstretched and address audience]

URIEL: Don't be afraid.

HANIEL: We bring you Good News of great joy for all people!

KEMUEL: Today in Bethlehem, your Messiah and Lord has been born.

URIEL: You will find the Baby Jesus snugly wrapped in cloths and lying in a manger.

ALL: Glory to God in the highest heaven, and peace to all people on earth!

KEMUEL: Okay angels: 1-2-3! *[strums guitar]*

[ANGELS sing "It was on a Starry Night" or other familiar Christmas song, encouraging audience to join in. If audience is moving to another scene, ISAIAH will quietly direct them onwards near end of song]

SCENE FIVE: Night, the stable with bright star above

[MUSIC as curtain pulls back to show manger scene with MARY, JOSEPH and the BABY. After some quiet moments, ISAIAH speaks softly]

ISAIAH: This is where we've been heading – to see our long-promised Messiah. God with us. King Jesus! I'll leave you to make your own way back to the future – I want to stay and worship this very special baby.

[MUSIC continues as ISAIAH kneels before the baby]

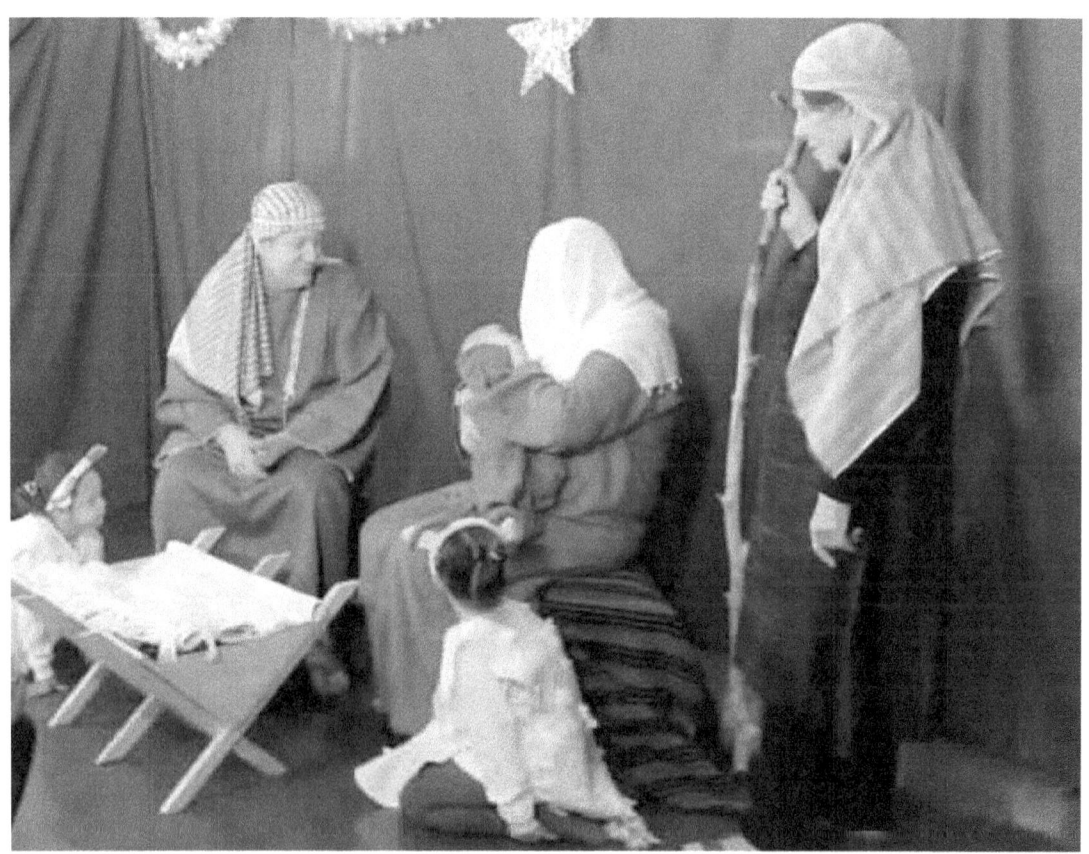

Production Notes for "A Very Special Baby"

STAGING: This was performed pre-Covid by having audience groups move past a series of small "theatres" made by curtaining off sections of the church, creating a unique experience for the viewers. ISAIAH is the guide who links the scenes and leads the audience forward. He will stand to one side observing as each scene is performed.

The drama could also be enacted in a larger auditorium, with quick scene changes. Middle Eastern drapes could provide a generic backdrop so only a few props would need carrying on.

ACTORS: There are 17 speaking parts, some of which can be taken by children, plus a few non-speaking parts. While having this many actors may seem overwhelming, most have only a few lines, so it's mainly daunting for the director! Two or more Isaiahs will be needed, if the audience is being led past the scenes in small groups.

At the end, people might be given a chance to write a prayer on a star and hang it on the nearby Christmas tree, after which stewards direct them out.

Alternatively, some of the scenes could be performed separately over Sundays in Advent. In that case, parts could double up, with the maximum number of actors needed being seven.

Individual scenes could also be performed in youth group, setting up a discussion about who Jesus is, why his birth was so significant and what this has to do with our lives today.

PROPS:
Desert scene:
gold, frankincense, myrrh
decorated box for carrying the gifts
camel props
Persian carpet on floor to indicate space of tent
campfire made from sticks of wood over a camping lantern covered with red
    cellophane

Inn scene:
old-fashioned broom for innkeeper's wife

Hillside:
shepherd crook
campfire

Angels:
guitar

Stable:
manger

DRAMAS FOR CHURCH OR YOUTH GROUP

THE BOX

SCENE: Onstage a large purple box labelled THE BOX

Mo
Kezzie
Hannah
Dylan
Alix
Homeless person
Bin Collector 1
Bin Collector 2

[ENTER MO and KEZZIE]

MO: Kezzie, I've been wondering – do you ever think about – it?

KEZZIE: About what?

MO: You know. *[nodding in direction of Box]* The Box.

KEZZIE: *[embarrassed, not looking at Box]* Oh! Well, erm, I don't think there really is a Box. That's just a myth. You don't believe in The Box, do you?

MO: I do, I really do. Only, well, it's just so – purple! And square. I wish there was more to it than that.

[ENTER HANNAH and DYLAN, ALL greet each other]

KEZZIE: Let's ask them. What do you two think about, the, uh –

DYLAN: What?

HANNAH: I bet you're talking about The Box, aren't you!

MO: Yeah, we are.

HANNAH: Oh, I love The Box! *[gives it a cuddle]* It's so warm and fuzzy. I can tell it all my problems – like yesterday, I told it how my best friend said she didn't want to be my best friend any more, 'cos she has a new best friend, but her new best friend used to be my best friend before we fell out, and –

KEZZIE: *[disgusted]* You're just talking to yourself!

DYLAN: And then what? Your problems are solved?

HANNAH: Of course! Or at least, I don't think about them any more. For a while.

DYLAN: That sounds good, let me try it! *[speaks to Box]* Hey Box, I have a big problem: I took money my mum gave me for a notebook and spent it on sweets. I need to have a fiver right away, before she finds out!

[KEZZIE rolls her eyes. MO, HANNAH and DYLAN all stare intently at The Box for a while, but nothing happens]

KEZZIE: See? I told you, there isn't any Box! You're just imagining things.

DYLAN: Maybe that's good. 'Cos if there really was a Box, it might want to tell me how to live my life, and I can't be doing with that!

MO: I don't think you used the right tone.

DYLAN: What was wrong with my tone?

MO: It wasn't very respectful. You should have said, *[in a holy tone]* "O kind and gracious Box" –

HANNAH: Maybe you didn't have enough faith. You won't get anything out of The Box if you don't have lots and lots of faith.

[ALIX runs onstage]

ALIX: *[furious]* Where – is – that – Box? Let me at it!

MO: What's wrong?

ALIX: I've tried so hard to be everything The Box would want me to be. I wear my "What Would The Box Do" bracelet. I talk to The Box every night. I thought The Box was on my side!

HANNAH: What happened?

ALIX: What *didn't* happen! I *didn't* make the hockey team and the cat was sick all over my English homework! Everything's going wrong, and it's all the fault of that Box!

[ALIX gives The Box a kick, MO, HANNAH and DYLAN react in shock]

HOMELESS PERSON: *[from within Box]* Ow, stop that!

ALIX: Oh! I didn't realise The Box had feelings!

HP: Of course I have feelings!

[ENTER BIN COLLECTORS 1&2]

BC 1: Back off, please. We're taking this away.

DYLAN: You can't take that!

BC 2: Why not?

HANNAH: It's The Box!

BC 1: We can see that, luv. Can't leave it out on the street, can we?

BC 2: Come on George, you grab that side.

[BIN COLLECTORS lift up Box to reveal HOMELESS PERSON clutching a blanket and carry Box off, followed by MO and HANNAH]

MO: Come back! You can't take our Box!

HANNAH: Who will I tell my problems to?

ALIX: *[staring at homeless person, puzzled]* But, The Box is –

HP: *[standing]* Where I sleep. It's been fun listening to people talk about "The Box".

DYLAN: But we always thought The Box was, well –

KEZZIE: God! Obviously you were wrong.

HP: Obviously. God doesn't live in a box.

KEZZIE: What did I tell you!

DYLAN: If The Box isn't God, then how do we find out what God is like?

HP: Try using your brains! And your heart. *[huddles on floor to one side and pulls blanket over him/herself]*

[HANNAH and MO return without The Box, looking depressed]

ALIX: Maybe she's right. Maybe God doesn't belong in a box.

HANNAH: How can we get him out?

DYLAN: That boy/girl said to use our brains and our heart.

MO: Remember what our youth leader said? If we want to know what God is like, we should look at Jesus.

KEZZIE:	Huh. So, what was Jesus like?
HANNAH:	Well, he loved all sorts of people, no matter what they were like.
ALIX:	He calmed a massive storm. So he's really powerful.
MO:	I believe he was God's Son.
HANNAH:	Do you think Jesus really hears us when we pray?
HP:	*[sits up]* Of course he does! Only he's not a machine where you put in your requests and get out whatever you want.
DYLAN:	I guess, Jesus sees everything I get up to.
HP:	And he still loves you.
ALIX:	I know I shouldn't blame him for everything that goes wrong in my life.
MO:	I want to get to know him better!
HP:	That makes him happy. As for you, Kezzie –
KEZZIE:	What? You know my name?
HP:	Of course. In your heart, you know there's something to this Jesus business. Look into it!

[HP lies down and pulls blanket over him/herself. During next lines he/she exits, leaving blanket behind]

KEZZIE:	Uh, okay, I guess I should.
DYLAN:	What do you say, we don't put God back in that Box!
ALL:	Good idea! Right! etc. *[ALL exit chanting]* No more Box! No more Box!

[KEZZIE turns to wave to HP, but he/she has disappeared. KEZZIE stares in astonishment, then runs after the others]

ADAM AND EVIE

SCENE: Garden of Eden, with a bench and caged snake

Adam
Evie
Zoo boss
Snake
Chorus of butterflies
Lion
Lamb

[LAMB on bench, teasing snake by pretending to paw it. SNAKE hisses and pretends to strike. LAMB jumps back, giggling]

LAMB: You're in a cage, and I'm not!

SNAKE: *[chuckles falsely. He uses fake nice voice throughout]* I love being behind bars. Wouldn't trade it for the world. *[gives muted evil hiss]*

[ENTER LION]

LION: Hi, Lambie!

LAMB: Hi, Lion! Let's play!

LION: Sure!

[ENTER BUTTERFLY CHORUS]

CHORUS: Can we play too?

LAMB: Come on!

[ANIMALS and BUTTERFLIES skip around, playing together]

SNAKE: I'd love to play with you. We can play skip-rope and I'll be the rope!

LAMB: Okay!

[CHORUS twitter fearfully. LAMB paws at lock of cage but can't open it. ANIMALS continue playing. Enter ADAM and EVIE with brooms. They begin sweeping energetically]

EVIE: You know, Adam, I love taking care of the zoo. It's so much fun being here with the animals in this beautiful garden.

ADAM:	And there's hardly any dirt – not much work to it.
EVIE:	Except cleaning that cage. *[sniffs the air near the snake's cage]* Phew!
ADAM:	Too right Evie, talk about a pong!
SNAKE:	You could let me out, you know. Then you could give my cage a really good clean. *[hisses softly]*

[CHORUS flutter around upset, gather to one side, listening]

EVIE:	We can't do that. The boss said not to!
ADAM:	That's right.
SNAKE:	No he didn't.
CHORUS:	Yes he did!
SNAKE:	You misunderstood! He said to put me in my cage at night. He lets me out in the daytime.
CHORUS:	No he doesn't!
SNAKE:	My cage wouldn't get so dirty if you'd let me out occasionally.
EVIE:	That's a good point.
ADAM:	I'm not sure –
CHORUS:	Listen to him! *[pointing to Adam]*
SNAKE:	Besides, it's not fair! All the other animals are free. The boss wouldn't want you to be unfair, would he?
EVIE:	No. He wouldn't want *that*. Adam, the boss wants us to be fair, doesn't he?
ADAM:	You're right, he does.
CHORUS:	Don't listen to him! *[pointing to Adam]*
EVIE:	Maybe we should let the snake out.
CHORUS:	Oh no you shouldn't!
ADAM:	Maybe we shouldn't.
EVIE:	I think we should.

ADAM: Oh go on, you do it.

EVIE: Okay.

CHORUS: We can't look!

[CHORUS cover their eyes, trembling. EVIE unlocks the cage and steps back. SNAKE slithers quickly out]

CHORUS: Look out, he's dangerous!

[ADAM and EVIE jump onto bench]

SNAKE: Good idea. I'm dangerous, you know.

[SNAKE bites ADAM on the heel]

ADAM: Ouch!

LAMB: *[to Lion]* Let's play!

LION: Okay! *[begins to chase Lamb]*

SNAKE: *[to Lion]* You don't *play* with lambs any more.

LION: I don't?

SNAKE: No – no – no. Lambs are delicious. And you are very hungry.

LION: Ooo, I'm very hungry. Oh look – lamb chops!

[LAMB baa's as LION chases it offstage. SNAKE slithers away, hissing and chuckling. Enter ZOO BOSS]

BOSS: What's going on?

EVIE: *[innocently]* The snake got out somehow!

CHORUS: She *let* him out!

BOSS: *[sadly]* Did you do this, Evie?

EVIE: The snake was really convincing!

SNAKE: *[pops his head out]* I was really convincing!

BOSS: Adam, where were you when this happened?

ADAM: Evie was really convincing.

CHORUS: They were really convincing – but wrong!

EVIE: *[to Boss]* But, you want us to be fair –

BOSS: I had one simple rule for my zoo, and you broke it. I'm really sorry....

[BOSS reaches out his arms towards ADAM and EVIE, shaking his head sadly. After a moment they climb down from bench and exit, crying]

CHORUS: This is the end!

BOSS: This not the end. I'll still be with them, even if they don't see me. Later on, in another place, I'll take care of that snake!

CHORUS: When? Where?

BOSS: Years from now, in another garden. Don't worry, this is just the beginning!

OUT OF OUR COMFORT(S) ZONE

SCENE: Interior of one-room house in Cambodian village. Bench where Grannie sits, curtain behind which parents sleep

Bethany
Jamie
Auntie [Ming]
Uncle [Boo]
Thida [girl, pronounced 'Teeda']
Sophea [girl, pronounced 'Sopeea']
Grannie [Yay]

[BETHANY downstage, recording video on phone, others in house doing tasks]

BETHANY: It's our first day in the village in Cambodia, and it's all so strange. The family we're staying with are really nice. They all live in this one room – I don't know where we'll sleep! I have to remember to call the mother 'Ming' which means Auntie. The dad is 'Boo'! That sounds funny but it means Uncle. And the Grannie is 'Yay'! Oh, I forgot to ask where the loo is!

BETHANY: *[goes into house]* Excuse me, Ming? Where is your toilet?

MING: Toe – let? What is this?

BETHANY: Erm, you know, when you need to go....

BOO: No problem, we have place! Bet-any, you must not think we are ignorant village people. No, we buy for you – wait – *[goes behind curtain, comes out with roll of toilet paper]* Here you are!

BETHANY: Oh that's cool, thanks Boo! Now, where do I go?

MING: Out in the field, Bet-any, Boo will show you.

BETHANY: In the field? But – aren't there snakes?

[SOPHEA and THIDA giggle]

BOO: I guard you, so no snakes or water buffalo will bother you.

JAMIE: Water buffalo?

SOPHEA: Not dangerous. Like friendly cows.

BETHANY: Uh, okay.

[BOO leaves, followed hesitantly by BETHANY]

JAMIE: Ming, this chicken stew looks really good. I'm starving!

YAY: Jay-mee, you do not know what is starving! In my family were ten people. Every day we had one bowl of rice, that was all.

JAMIE: That sounds terrible!

MING: Today we have killed our chicken for you, our honoured guests. Makes very nice stew. Tomorrow we have rice, maybe with fish heads.

JAMIE: Uh, okay, thanks.

YAY: My sisters and brothers, all starve. I am only one left. It was a very bad time in our country, soldiers kill many people too.

THIDA: Mah, Jay-mee can help me water the vegetables.

JAMIE: I'll be glad to help.

MING: Good, take buckets. Fields very dry now, crops die if we do not water.

[THIDA gets double buckets, places them across her own and JAMIE's shoulders]

JAMIE: How far is the water?

THIDA: Water in our village pond all dried up. We go to next village – maybe two-three miles?

JAMIE: Right.

SOPHEA: Yay, I will get more mulberry leaves for your silkworms.

YAY: Here, go quickly. *[hands basket to Sophea]* The worms eat, eat, eat now. Soon they will spin cocoons. Then we make silk, show you how, Jay-mee.

JAMIE: Thank you.

YAY: Be careful, only walk on path.

JAMIE: Are there snakes?

MING: Not because of snakes.

JAMIE: That's a relief!

THIDA:	Snakes are everywhere. But if you go off the path, you might step on a landmine.
YAY:	The bad soldiers, they did that – buried mines under the earth. You step on – BOOM!

[JAMIE, THIDA and SOPHEA exit. BETHANY runs back in, screaming, followed by BOO holding toilet paper and a small snake]

BETHANY:	A snake! It almost bit me!
BOO:	Only small snake, not dangerous! Maybe we put in pot with chicken, no?
BETHANY:	No! I mean, please don't.

[CAMBODIAN MUSIC indicates passing of time. ALL lie down to sleep on the floor except JAMIE who goes downstage to record on phone]

JAMIE:	Well, it's four in the morning and I've hardly slept a wink. That one scrawny chicken had to feed all of us. Other than that, it was just rice and more rice. I can hear my stomach shrinking! The geckoes in the roof make a chirping noise that goes on and on.
	I can't believe what their Grannie had to go through when she was young. These people have so little, but they're so generous with us, I can hardly take it in. I'm going to try and get a few hours of sleep.

[JAMIE goes back to lie on floor; ROOSTER crows. ALL except BETHANY and JAMIE get up]

JAMIE:	No!
BETHANY:	Muurmph?
SOPHEA:	Get up, Bet-any. You can help us make breakfast!
THIDA:	Then we go to church. Come on!
JAMIE:	*[hopefully]* What's for breakfast?
MING:	Rice.

[JAMIE groans]

SOPHEA:	Mah, we have guests, so can we have sour melon stew instead?

JAMIE: Rice sounds fine! I love rice! *[gets up]* Get up, Bethany!

BETHANY: What time is it? It's still dark!

JAMIE: Half past four. And we're having rice for breakfast.

[BETHANY groans, then gets up. ALL sit on floor and bow heads]

BOO: Thank you Lord Jesus, for loving us, and giving us good food every day. Amen. *[looks up]* I got special treat yesterday from the market. Look! *[holds out paper containing fried giant spiders]*

BETHANY: *[screams]* Those are spiders!

BOO: Giant spiders, crispy fried, you try?

[JAMIE and BETHANY shake their heads. JAMIE is trying to make bowl of rice last a long time]

BETHANY: I think I'll skip breakfast. I want to have a shower and do my make-up.

MING: No time for that! We eat quick and go to church.

JAMIE: And just how far is this church?

BOO: Not far, maybe five-six miles?

THIDA: Yay, I hope your legs get better soon, so you can go to church again.

[ALL exit except YAY]

YAY: *[gets up, walks with stick downstage]* I hope the English children don't find our church too strange. Well, I will go pick bananas, we can fry them for our dinner. *[She exits to rear]*

[CAMBODIAN WORSHIP MUSIC, which fades as ALL return, YAY carrying bananas. ALL start preparing food while Bethany moves downstage to record on phone]

BETHANY: We walked seven miles to church and back, plus church lasted for hours! You wouldn't believe how hot it is here. Good thing I didn't put on any make-up – it would have just run down my face. I'm so hungry I'm about to faint, but I had to come and record before I eat.

Ming and Boo and their family have nothing, but they're so happy. They're the only Christians in the village, but it seems like Jesus is so real to them, like he's right here with them. Before I left the UK, I was begging my parents for an iPhone. But my stuff doesn't seem so important any more. Being here has made me look at happiness in a new way. Wonder if I'll remember all this when I get back home, and make some changes. I hope I will!

[BETHANY returns to house and ALL bow their heads in prayer]

BE KIND, REWIND

SCENE: "Trainee Angel School"; a small, decorated cabinet visible at rear. On one side a few chairs and lectern to indicate church; on the other, "Corner Shop"

Head Angel
Trainee Angels 1-2-3
Persons 1-2
Shopkeeper

HEAD ANGEL:	Hello Trainee Angels, and welcome to your first day of Angel School! I'm the Head Angel here. You've each been assigned to a person.
ANGEL 1:	*[raises hand]* Miss?
HEAD ANGEL:	Don't call me Miss! What is it?
ANGEL 1:	How are we meant to help our person?
HEAD ANGEL:	You can help them in practical ways, such as preventing an accident. Or you can make an accident be less serious than it might be. Any questions?
ANGEL 3:	What if they're about to do something bad? Can we stop them?
HEAD ANGEL:	No. And that brings me to the main rule of Angel School. When it comes to their behaviour, you *never interfere*. Understand?
ANGELS:	Never interfere.
HEAD ANGEL:	Good! You can't change how they behave.
ANGELS:	We can't change how they behave.
HEAD ANGEL:	That's between them and God. They have to learn to trust him. Now, off you go!

[PERSON 1 enters from behind audience, wearing a hoodie with hood down]

ANGEL 1:	That one's mine!
ANGEL 2:	Look, she doesn't see that car!

[ANGEL 1 runs down and grabs PERSON 1 to hold her back, SOUND of screeching tyres. ANGEL 1 returns, they all high-five. Meanwhile PERSON 1 puzzled, looking around to see what was holding her]

ANGEL 2: Here comes mine!

[PERSON 2 enters, goes to Corner Shop, followed by PERSON 1]

PERSON 1: *[to PERSON 2]* Hiya!

PERSON 2: Oh, hi.

SHOPKEEPER: Mind you don't touch anything! You touch, you buy, geddit?

PERSON 2: I'll have a bag of mint humbugs, please.

PERSON 1: I love humbugs! *[looking expectantly at PERSON 2]*

[SHOPKEEPER holds out sweets, but PERSON 2 doesn't take them]

SHOPKEEPER: Well, do you want them, or not? I haven't got all day!

PERSON 2: Sorry, I don't want them after all.

PERSON 1: You don't?

PERSON 2: I'll take that bunch of flowers, please.

SHOPK: Whatever.

[PERSON 2 pays for flowers, walks away. PERSON 1 follows, disappointed]

PERSON 1: Why didn't you want the humbugs?

PERSON 2: I really did – but then I remembered, my Gran's feeling so ill today, I think these flowers might cheer her up.

[PERSON 1 shrugs and scoffs]

PERSON 2: If you must know, I kinda felt like God was reminding me about my Gran.

[PERSON 1 rolls eyes. PERSON 2 exits. PERSON 1 puts hood up, returns to shop where she steals some sweets, then runs off down aisle]

SHOPKEEPER: Oi! Come back here!

ANGEL 1: Put those back!

[ANGEL 1 starts to run after her but ANGEL 2 and ANGEL 3 hold him back]

ANGEL 2 and **3**:	Never interfere!
ANGEL 1:	I don't see why not. I go to all that trouble to save her life, and then she just steals!
ANGEL 2:	It's not our business how they live their lives.
ANGEL 3:	Like the Head Angel said, they have to learn to trust God.
ANGEL 1:	Seems like it leaves too much to chance. You know – I've heard a rumour, God has this emergency remote control –
ANGEL 3:	Oh yeah, I heard about that. But he's the only one who gets to use it.
ANGEL 1:	Right. So, what I'm thinking is – we could sort of, borrow God's remote for a bit?
ANGEL 2:	*[shocked]* That would be stealing!
ANGEL 1:	No, that would be *borrowing*.
ANGEL 3:	Maybe just to try it out for a few minutes....
ANGEL 1:	Wonder where he keeps it?
ANGEL 2:	You guys are going to get your wings clipped, if you aren't careful!

[ANGEL 1 and ANGEL 3 find cabinet and take out remote control]

ANGEL 3:	Here comes your person!
ANGEL 2:	Stealing again!

[PERSON 1 returns to shop, steals more sweets and starts to sneak off]

ANGEL 1:	Not this time!
SHOPKEEPER:	Oi! You! Come back with that!

[PERSON 1 runs off down aisle, with shopkeeper chasing]

ANGEL 1:	Watch this! Freeze!

[ANGEL 1 pushes button and they freeze]

ANGEL 3:	That was cool! Now what?
ANGEL 1:	Let's rewind and play it again!

[ANGEL 1 pushes buttons; SHOPKEEPER and PERSON 1 rewind into their original positions, PERSON 1 replaces sweets]

SHOPKEEPER: *[sounding mechanical]* Hello, dear child. I love children coming into my shop and touching the sweets.

PERSON 1: *[sounding mechanical]* You have such delicious things here. I don't have any money today, I just want to stand here and smell the wonderful aroma.

SHOPKEEPER: *[sounding mechanical]* Of course. I am always glad to have such fine girls in my shop.

ANGEL 1: Freeze!

[ANGEL 1 pushes remote and they freeze. HEAD ANGEL appears]

ANGEL 1: Something was wrong.

ANGEL 3: They sounded funny.

ANGEL 2: That's because you just *forced* them to be nice.

HEAD ANGEL: What's going on here?

ANGEL 1: Nothing!

HEAD ANGEL: What's that in your hand?

ANGEL 1: It's, erm –

ANGEL 3: We were just walking past God's cabinet and there it was!

HEAD ANGEL: Only God gets to touch that, as you well know!

ANGEL 1,2 and 3: Sorry, really sorry.

[During next speech, HEAD ANGEL takes remote]

ANGEL 2: Why doesn't God *make* people behave? He could use his remote control and everyone would be good all the time!

HEAD ANGEL: You've seen why. You wouldn't have people, you'd have machines. They have to choose for themselves to follow him.

ANGEL 1: But if I don't do something, my person will probably end up going to prison!

HEAD ANGEL:	*[pauses, thinking]* Look – I'll make an exception just this once and fast forward ten years. *[presses remote]* You might be surprised how things turn out.

[SHOPKEEPER moves to sit on chairs, along with PERSON 2. PERSON 1 removes hood and crosses to lectern]

PERSON 1:	Maybe when you see a minister like myself you think, "She must have been a really good kid growing up." But I wasn't. In fact, I used to steal sweets from the corner shop.
SHOPKEEPER:	*[to PERSON 2]* I remember her! She was that cheeky girl who always stole from me!
PERSON 2:	What happened to change her?
PERSON 1:	God was working in my heart all the time. I knew the way I was living was wrong. Finally, I asked him to forgive me and give me new life in Jesus, and he did!

[ANGELS reacting to this]

HEAD ANGEL:	Freeze!

[HEAD clicks remote, scene freezes]

HEAD ANGEL:	So, trainee angels, tell me what you've learned from this.
ANGEL 2:	I see, God's Spirit is speaking to people in their hearts.
HEAD ANGEL:	Good! What else?
ANGEL 3:	So, *they* have to choose if they'll listen and obey him.
ANGEL 1:	And if they do, then their lives will show it. Awesome!
HEAD ANGEL:	Excellent. Now, I'll just lock this away in a safe place –

[ANGEL 1 and ANGEL 3 look at each other, nod, grab the remote from HEAD ANGEL and start waving it at the people. ANGEL 2 rolls her eyes. PERSON 1, PERSON 2 and SHOPKEEPER perform random movements until HEAD ANGEL grabs the remote again. She clicks it off and shouts,]

HEAD ANGEL: THE END!

AN EASTER MEDITATION

"I REMEMBER …"

An old woman, Abigail

I remember. I am old now, but still I remember that night unlike any other night….

The room is dark, shuttered. Oil lamps on the low table make points of light on the men's faces. My little brother Benjamin and I are the only children. We love tagging along with Uncle, watching him do miracles, listening to his stories.

Andrew sees us. "Abigail, you and Benjamin should go home now," he whispers.

"Come on, Abigail," Benjamin says, "we'd better go," but I shake my head. "Let Uncle send us away, if he doesn't want us here! I want to hear some stories!"

But tonight, in the closed-off upper room, with his friends reclining around the table, Uncle doesn't tell stories. Maybe we should have gone home after all. He's almost frowning, and it promises to be boring. None of the disciples is blind or lame or leprous – there's nothing to heal, no demons are going to be cast out, as far as I can see.

Uncle recites the blessing to begin the Passover meal. Benjamin is the youngest child here, so Uncle calls him forward.

"Benjamin, you may ask the Passover question."

My brother's eyes sparkle as he says proudly, "Why is this night different from all other nights?"

But instead of answering in the traditional way, Uncle talks of things I don't understand. Betrayal. Glory. And love – again and again he speaks of love.

I watch the men's faces. Thomas, always frowning, with his everlasting questions. "Why? Where? How?" Philip so solemn, wanting to believe but unsure. "Show us the Father," he says. Uncle smiles. "You're looking at him!" Philip's dark eyes grow round as copper coins.

And there's Simon Peter. Uncle tells Peter he will deny even knowing him. Peter's open face is a picture of wounded pride. Uncle is his closest friend! How could Peter ever turn his back on him? It's almost as if Uncle is *trying* to upset everyone tonight.

"You're going to be doing even greater works than I have, after I'm gone," he says. He means to be encouraging, but we all stare in dismay.

Gone! Where is he going? The men burst out with protests.

"I'm not abandoning you. You're all so quick to worry! My life will be bubbling up from within you. Just wait until you see the miracles you'll be doing!"

Peter wipes his face on his sleeve. "I want to do these miracles, Master!"

Uncle smiles, but his eyes look sad. By now my brother is curled up on the floor, snoring and I'm sitting next to him yawning, but desperate not to miss anything. Uncle's eyes move from face to face round the room, as if he wants to hold each one in his mind after he goes. He speaks, and I've never heard him be so earnest.

"If you love me, you will obey me."

"We will, Master!" they all exclaim, and the oil flames flicker with the force of their breath.

"Good! Do you remember, what is the most important thing?"

The room is silent. Even Peter hesitates, for once.

"Well?"

Why don't they remember? He's said it over and over. I can't help myself; I stand up and shout it out. "It's love!"

Uncle smiles at me. "Abigail has said it! Love. Love for me, love for each other. Love for everyone you meet. But don't be anxious about this, for I'm sending you a special friend to help you. Take courage – you will need it, tonight of all nights."

I am pleased and proud of Uncle's praise. We sing a Passover song, and I should be joyful, but I sense unspoken fears beating in each heart. Something dreadful is about to happen. The meal is over; we go out into the clear night. And Uncle goes away, just as he promised. His awful going....

I have never forgotten that night. Or that smile, which lights my life every day, no matter how dark. From the man who was my beloved Uncle Jesus...who went away. And yet, he didn't! I remember....

Production Notes for "I Remember …"

STAGING: This could be read with the actor not visible to the audience, while showing appropriate images of the Upper Room scene. Alternatively, the scene could be performed by actors with Abigail as narrator.

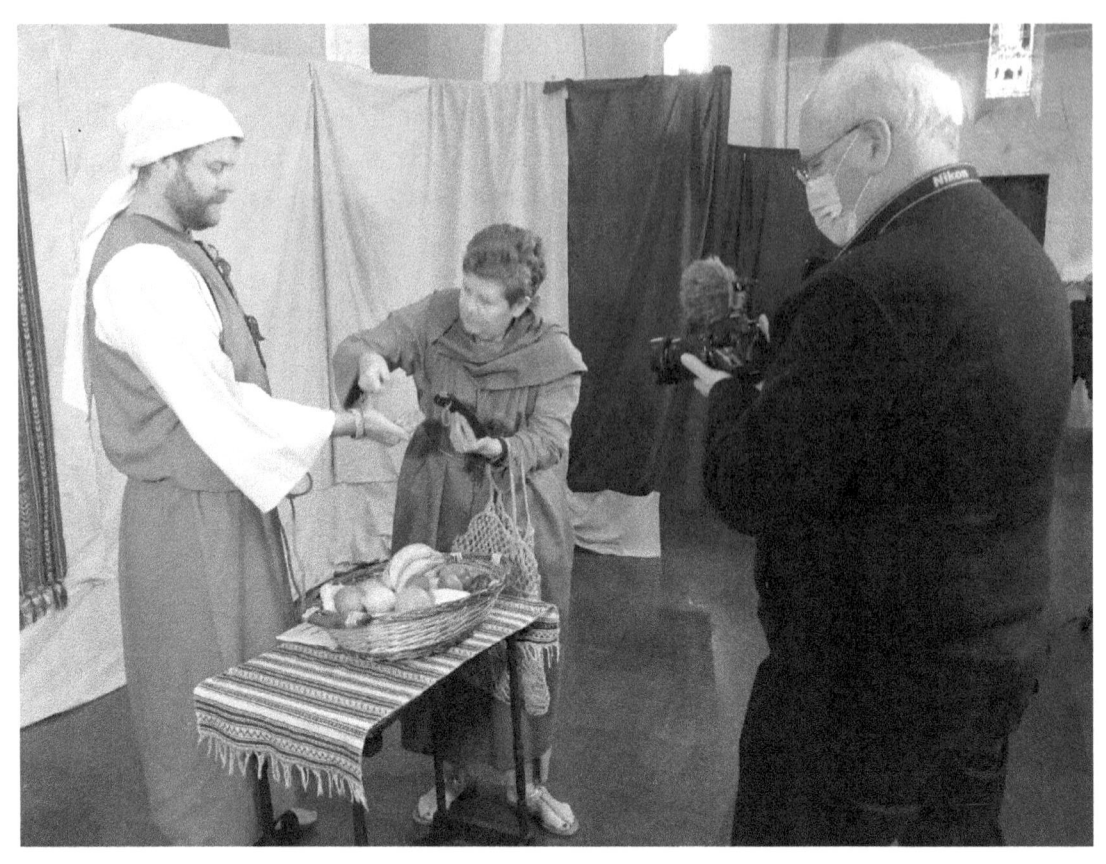

ABOUT THE AUTHOR

As a child in Texas, Donna loved cycling downhill with her mouth open; the combination of speed, skinned knees and swallowed grasshoppers gave her a sense of drama in the ordinary. At the age of eight she wrote, directed and performed her first play, a puppet show for her class.

Much later her one-act play "The Sun Porch" was chosen for a rehearsed reading in Stratford-upon-Avon. She has years of experience in writing and directing plays for young people in the UK, as well as Nativity dramas.

Donna's books are available from Amazon UK and Amazon US. She is currently working on poems, picture books and novels for children, and of course, her next Nativity script.

A Word from Donna

If your group enjoyed performing any of the plays in this book, I would love to hear about it. Please contact me via my website, www.donnavann.com

If you could take a moment to leave a review on Amazon, I would really appreciate it. Your positive feedback is so important, giving me the encouragement all authors need, as well as being helpful for prospective readers. Thank you so much!

www.ingramcontent.com/pod-product-compliance
Lightning Source LLC
Chambersburg PA
CBHW081919090526
44590CB00019B/3407